MOVING PRAYERS
AND
QUIET MEDITATIONS

Interfaith Prayers for the
Journey of Life

Anthea Ballam

For Jane

ISBN 978-0-9564245-0-1
Printed by Newman Thomson
Burgess Hill, West Sussex
www.newmanthomson.com

Designed by Sue Smallwood
Published by Rev Anthea Ballam
Copyright © 2009 Anthea Ballam

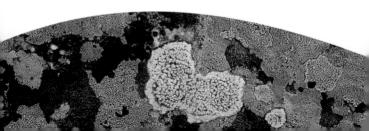

INTRODUCTION

The parallel between a lifetime and the journey of the spirit is an accepted concept in many cultures. The journey is celebrated from birth to death and during this time there will be moments when we may pray for ourselves, or others may pray for us. The life journey takes in all kinds of landscape – comedy, tragedy, moments of fear, uncertainties – from our first love and the excitement of marriage to family festivities, then old age and death. These prayers were written with such occasions in mind. For the most part they are intended to be spoken aloud, which is why the punctuation is open and airy.

It is hoped that you find this prayer book useful and also enjoy reading it.

Thank you.

THE PRAYERS

THE JOURNEY BEGINS

1: OPEN THE HEART

Open up
To the sky
To the sea
To your child
To your partner
To the world

Unfasten your soul
And hear the sweet song of a bird

When you step into the air
The breeze brushes your cheek like a lover
And when you stop and listen
The wind will call you
The rustling leaves
Will speak of tranquillity
Recalling water and the gentle tide

If you close your eyes
You will make a discovery
The world knows you are there

It knows you as a child
Or maybe an ancient tree
Holding a thousand spirits
In the loving embrace of your branches

When you hear these words of love
You will see the flower I gave you
You will breathe in its fragrance
Admire its beauty
While it rests in the palm of your hand
How fragile and delicate it seems
Open, perfect, light as a feather
Radiant as sunshine
Mysterious as a moonbeam

The flower is the wisdom of the heart
It grows in the garden of time without end
Nurtured by the One that cares for us
It is the force of love
The passion that made us all
In the enchanted garden of the universe

Open up and be blessed
Joining with the Spirit, in love,
as One

2: STARTING OUT

Take me with you
Angel of adventure
Hold my hand
Along the way

3: ANGEL INVOCATION

I summon you
To a desolate place
Home to a lonely, aged soul
Washed up on the shores of time
Poor as a church mouse
Grey as a ghost
Sadder than sorrow
Bring him company
Kindness, and the warmth of love

I summon you
To a heartbroken child
Whose parents
Were killed in war
Alone, she sits by the roadside

Clutching her only toy
She cries inconsolably
Sadder than sorrow
Give her compassion
And the beauty of your love

I summon you
To the fearful
To the lonely
To the neglected
To those who suffer
Ease their journeys
Through the terror of a world
Unbearable without you
Carry them in your arms
So that they may be healed
By the power
Of your divine grace and love

4: THE SOUND OF MY HEART

The sound of my heart
Is a song of the spirit
It beats in praise of the mother
It chants in thanks to the father
The song of my heart
Is my own
And yours
And yours
And yours
And all of us
Resonate in harmony
With each other

5: THANKS…

I cannot believe in a God who wants to be praised all the time. (Friedrich Nietzche)

Maybe… but who can resist thanking the One who created the blackbird and its exquisite song. Being spiritual and grateful is as natural as breathing.

Today I give thanks
Whether I feel like it
Or not

It's in the giving of thanks
I feel better

It's in the movement of a smile
I feel like smiling

It's in the singing of a song
I cheer up

It is in the laughing of a laugh
My troubles melt

Today I give thanks
And realise the world
Is amazing, after all

6: GREETING PASSION

I am open
To fervour
To harmony
 And peace

I see and distinguish
The darkness and light
Chaos and order
Beauty and mystery

I listen and hear
Silence and being
The world in movement
Turning mechanically
Under the sun and the moon

I feel
Love in motion
Myself and all things
Caught in the dance of life

With hands and heart
I hold the one I adore
Believing this to be
The moment of completion

For in love
True love
We paint everything
Hear the beauty
Touch the emotions
And feel divine passion

ARRIVING AND NEW ARRIVALS

7: WELCOME TO THE LIGHT

Let us honour the life-force of the family
The harmony within the house
The sheer fun that comes from growing things
From the smallest seed to the laughing babe
The magical joy and light we witness in this
sacred space
May all these powers combine
In the blessing of our new arrival to this world
And in so doing
Let us honour love
In time, now, and forever

8: THE GODPARENT'S PRAYER

The child that feels the wind
The child that hears the sound of the waves
The child that is radiant in the light of the sun
The child that is touched by the perfection
of the moon
Is truly blessed

Sweet one, you are adored and nurtured by
your parents
People of love and gentleness
You are loved and admired by your grandparents
But you and you alone
Are my godchild
And I have been entrusted with this role
And it is with respect
To all things sacred
That I will follow your steps
And spiritual pathways
Committing myself
To you
And the wishes of your parents
And the beloved spirit
That is the mother of all things
And the father of all things
Blessed Be

9: GRANDMOTHER'S PRAYER

When I gave birth to my child
It seemed unlikely I would stand here today
And rejoice in a new life, from that new life

Now we celebrate
A gift to the family

I give you my heart
As I gave my love to a newborn child
Years ago
I give you my love today
As a grandmother
For we both belong
To an indestructible pattern
Of family life
We both explored
Unknown paths
Trodden by knowing spirits

May you be strong
May you be happy
May you be wise
And may you have grace in all things
I seal my blessing with a kiss

MYSTERY, PEACE AND STRANGE MEETINGS

10: TO INSPIRATION

The most beautiful experience we can have is the mysterious. It is the fundamental emotion that stands at the cradle of true art and true science…

(Albert Einstein)

Take me to a palace
Deep and ever deeper in the cosmic gloom
There show me swirling clouds of colour
Purple as the robes of the wise
Red as fresh blood
Radiant as beaten gold

Carry me to the blue planet
To the gates of heaven
Luminous and lovely
And let me fly to Southern climes
To rest in olive groves
Serenaded by sweet birdsong

Open my soul to the song in a word
Let me sing a warbling note that floats afar
And falls like gentle rain
On a land of loveliness

Guide my hand to write
Words that shape the melodies of birdsong

Let the sailing ship of my soul
Float on a sunbeam
That I may paint a tapestry
Celebrating the harmony of life

In this way
I simply ask for the words
The music
And the splendour
To praise the grace
And the mystery of our world

11: SILENCE

Give me an empty bowl
That waits to be filled
Holding promise

In this moment
Who knows where to find it?
Hidden behind a beating heart?

Wherever one goes
Lone, alone
Sitting, moving, standing
It is elusive

Who needs it?
Yet without it
There is envy

It is given to those that cannot hear
People of the desert
The mountain priest

Is there anyone, anywhere
That owns such peace?
A dweller alone
In perfect stillness and seclusion

Let us rest in it
Let us cherish it
For it is ours
Yours and mine
In meditation
And for the asking
Bless this silence

12: PRAYER FOR NON BELIEVERS

I pray
For those
That can't pray
Who don't and won't believe
The wisdom and the spirit
Of ancient rocks and soaring trees
And sweeping oceans

I pray for those
That don't see
The story that unfolds
The pages turning
Who don't understand
The hurt, the holding and the taking
Of flesh and love and feelings
Memories and sensations
That own no words

I pray for those
That think that death
Is unnatural
For those grey minds
Who want to think
That sloppy science just says it all
And there is nothing left
For those who see a perfect sunset
As light – molecular activity
And refraction
And maybe natural selection too

I pray for those
Who think
The most delicious flower
Visited by a friendly bee
Is a genetic enterprise
A mathematical equation
A thing of concrete
A jot of matter
And spirit plays no part

Above all things
I pray
That one fine day
One of those good souls
Will hear the song of the blackbird
And it will bring tears to their eyes
And they'll understand
The perfection of spirit
And the inspiration of the divine

13: CELEBRATING FLOWERS

From the mysterious beauty
That is nature
Floats art
And in art
We celebrate divinity

There is a door
Both delicious and delicate
Coloured and fashioned
Beyond man's hand
It is a thing of spirit
and physical precision
And it is open to the bee
Not so much an invitation to dine
As a suggestion to 'taste' the nectar

And with this immense concept
Barely an inch from top to toe
There are seeds of greatness
Walls more delicate than paper
Proportions and the rules
Implicit in the temple of Athena

The Santa Maria Della Salute
Entrances better engineered
Than doors that open onto Fifth Avenue
Designs more fun than the elegance
Of a Regency Crescent.

In the mysterious beauty
That is nature
There is art
And in art
We celebrate
The glory of divinity

14: BALANCE

The light of life
The love of life
The soul of life
The mind of life
Are ours

Black and white
Day and night
Joyless and joyful
Weakened and healed
Wild and tame
They are with us
And we nurture them all

The beauty
The wisdom
The eternity
Of this world
Are within us

And so we are blessed

15: LOVING PROTECTION

Blessed spirit
I open my heart to you
Asking you to protect me
From those forces
That cross the mysterious pathways
Of my understanding

With each step along the way
I am touched by your radiance
Your love holds and protects me
And all fears are overcome

With each step taken
The gift of understanding
Shines on the gentle path of healing
Revealing wisdom, truth and harmony

MARRIAGE AND THE DIVINE

16: WEDDING PRAYER

Let us thank the Divine
For the perfection of two
For man and woman
For summer and winter
Day and night
Sun and moon
And all things in balance
That have been so
Since the beginning of time

The Beloved gave us two
In love, in life, and in nature
From the birds that fly
To the deer that run through the long grass
From the joy of young lovers
To the tender romance of the old

In cold lands and warm
Both near and far
The beauty of two
Husband and wife
Is strong and sublime
From the poorest humble home

To the most glorious palace
We celebrate marriage
And the sheer joy of true love

And with this sacred knowledge
Let us hold two thoughts in our hearts
Let us remember
That there is no one
Not one single soul
That walks alone on this earth
For God's angel is always with us
And let us remember
That this blessed moment
This sacred union of man and wife
Is a divine ritual
A celebration of the perfection of two
And their love for each other

For it is love, such as theirs
That opens the gates
To a realm of beauty and joy
Shared with family and friends
Blessed with happiness and laughter

Which is why we offer
Our thanks for this most sacred day
And this most sacred world
And the God of love
That loves us all

17: TO THE UNIVERSAL DIVINITY

I call upon the One
And the spirits and souls
Both visible and invisible
Great and small
That embody the forces
Of love and wisdom

I ask you
To love us
Care for us
Heal us
And sanctify us
For it is you
Above all things
We love
With all our hearts
And all our minds

May this blessing triumph
And the light of life
Be with us
Now and for always

18: THE GREAT SPIRIT *(Based on the Lord's Prayer)*

Great spirit
You are in us and around us
Above us and below us
Sacred and mysterious
In presence and name
This world is yours
And all that unfolds
Here and beyond
Is seen and manifest
For it is yours
As we are you
Nurture and care for us
And gift us with wisdom
To forgive and be forgiven
Let us not be weak
Or tempted to wander from the way
But carry us from the shadows
That we may walk
In the glorious light of your love

DEATH AND DEPARTURE

19: PRAYER OF DEPARTURE

It is the hour of the final journey
The moment of release
When your soul bids farewell
Leaving us in this world

This is your journey
Just as it was when you arrived
Now you will recall the return
For you have travelled this path before
It is the voyage of destiny

In this moment
When you and I are together
The material gives way to spirit
And your spirit
Is set free beyond the elements of earth
Now you can cast off the old
Leaving behind a husk, a shell
In a world we once shared

Here in our time and place
We see your departure
And share the last steps
And in this hour and beyond

We recollect your essence
Cherishing you
In a thousand moments and memories

Now we make our declaration and invocation
May your journey be sweet
May the way be loving
May the path be joyful
While we who remain on earth
Hold you
Like the most perfect flower
In our heart of hearts

20: FUNERAL READING

The door has closed
And you have gone
Leaving recollections
Of shared laughter
Floating across sunny days

Static we wait
In a sad house of life

Prisoners of reality
But we must learn
That the past
The laughter and the light
Are all great gifts
Painted in *joie de vivre*
Prizes we have to grasp
at this moment
Loving memories of you

And even now
On this sad day of mourning
So many souls
Here and now
Will feel and know
That we will meet again
That doors will open
Making loss mere illusion

Then this hour
That is so real today
Will pass, healed by time
Strengthened by love
Served by compassion
Lifted by understanding

21: DO NOT DESPAIR

Do not despair
Though you hear the cries of suffering and
sadness around you
Though you walk through the valley of death
with fear in your heart
Do not despair

Do not despair
If the one you love has been taken from you
If the divine flower of life has been extinguished
Do not despair

In the darkest hour
In the moment of empty desolation
There shines a light
You may not see it, but it is there
It is the light of the One that made you
The One that made your beloved
And the One that shaped this world

In the world of shadows there is the seed of light
So when you step into the gloom
Do not be afraid
A hand will guide you
It is my hand
It is the hand of your angel
It is the hand of the One that made us
Bringing us together in this moment
Now and forever

More glorious than hope
More radiant than joy
We are loved
We are at one with the One

We will walk from the darkness together
into the light
Knowing that darkness and light are
within us and around us
We are beings from a world of summer
and winter, day and night
Put aside fear and sadness
So that we may be healed
By the spirit of all things
Now and forever

22: PRAYER FOR THE GIFTED, NOW GONE

In the poetry and music of nature
We see art and share it
You believed in a world soul
Embodied in beauty, form and meaning
And you celebrated the glory that is art
Now we celebrate your life
And rejoice in the divine
That brought you into our lives

In everything
There is divinity
It's all about us
It's in the memory of you
It's in the pleasure of remembering you
It's in the song of the wind
It's in the flight of the bird
It's in this magic place
Where we will put to rest
The last trace
Of your physical remains

And in this sacred moment of ritual
We ask that you and the divine bless us
Just as we bless you and the divine

We think of you with love
A fine, mysterious and delicate wall
Stands between us and you
It's merely an illusion that there is any barrier
at all

The divine force of love knows no barriers
The divine power of love fears no death
And remembering this
We celebrate your life today, knowing
In all things
There is divinity

HEALING AND THE HEALER

23: IN THE HOUR OF NEED

Bless me divinity
For in this hour
I need you

Bless me divinity
For I have been afflicted
My body suffers
And my mind is not well

In the darkest hours
I am wracked with pain
Fearful and despairing
I care nothing
For today or tomorrow

I ask only
That I am relieved
Of the darkness in my soul
Shadowy and frightening

Bless me divinity
For in this hour
I call for you

I cry out to your angels
And your glorious radiant power
That will make me strong
So that I may live
To fight
And fight to live

24: THE HARMONY OF HEALING

Where there is silence
There is harmony
It is the sound of your heart pounding
The symphony of lungs breathing
The song of the spirit
Flowing on the waters of the soul

Where there is harmony
There is silence
Listen for the resonance
A small song brushes the air
Sweeping across an open plain
Swooping and diving
A winged spirit

In the quiet of the cosmos
And the still of the night
The earthly breeze moves
And comes to rest
On desert sands
And then you must listen

Such harmonies are yours
Skin against skin
Muscle on bone
The winged horse treading the air
The duet of man and bird
All these are yours

Breathe – and hear the sea
Walk and hear movement
Move and hear the universe
In stillness and with sound

Where there is silence
There is harmony

25: PRAYER FOR THE HEALER

Change this day
With your love

Touch the hearts
Of those you meet
With a tender thought

Bless the downhearted
The lonely and dejected
With a beautiful wish
For you have the gift
To understand suffering

It's the most gentle hands
Of calm and compassion
Serenity and service
That hold the power of the universe
The power to heal

And when things are calm
And waters are tranquil under the moon
Don't forget
It's not enough to care for us
You must love yourself
And care for yourself
In equal measure
With equal love

So today,
I bask in the warmth of the sun
And celebrate with all things made well
By you and your guiding spirit.

MOTHER, FATHER, SUN AND MOON

26: PRAYER FOR THE MOTHER

The mother is the beloved spirit
The divinity lives through her

We rest in the warmth of her love
Her patient steps echo on dusty paths
Yet the immensity of the cosmos
Will not possess her
From the beginning to the end of time

She alone takes the hand of her child
Guiding each faltering step towards tomorrow
She alone nurtures and loves
With a calm tenderness
Her gentle touch heals
Her smile brings forgiveness
From the beginning to the end of time

She above all
Will carry her brood from danger
Without thought for herself
Soaring spirit of the sky
Earth mother, soul mother
She holds us close to her heart
Where once we heard the music of life

Her gift is love
For she is sacred
The divinity lives through her

Blessed is the mother
For she is gentle in grace
And blessed are we
Her children
That cherish her memory
In time
In place
In life
And in death
Today, tomorrow and forever

27: FOR THE FATHER

He was ours
In his belonging
A man and a boy
With a huge heart
Loving and strong
Full of understanding

Offspring grew
And he was proud
Sometimes patient
And sometimes not

At the centre of us all
He showed true affection
Unexpected sweetness
And sometimes anger
Now his smile is captive
In our memories

His humour shared
He gave so much of himself
And kept so much to himself

We honour his lasting love
His legacy of strength
That will be carried
By his loving offspring

Blessed is the head of the house
The partner and father
Who cared for so many
Who laughed with us all
Mixing fondness with wisdom
And blessed are they
That knew and loved him

28: THE SUN IS OUR FATHER

The sun is our father
He smiles on us
The moon is our mother
We are her children
This world is our world
It is a gift

Under the smile of the sun
Worship at the altar of the undivided
Under the moon
Dream on the mystery of mysteries

In dreams we fly
In life hurry
Take this moment to stroll
Harmonious paths of learning
Catch a falling star
Make a wish

Those divided
Let them be complete
Those that are reviled
Let them be loved

Make our star shine
Without blemish
May the moon weave
Her loving magic
So that we are blessed
And healed
And gain understanding

29: THE GODDESS GUIDES ME

The goddess guides us
Revealing the miracle of this world

She dances on the wings of the butterfly
She glides on the whisper
Of the summer trees

The green downs are her cloak
The waters of the wild sea
Are her domain

But we have failed her
We have forgotten her glorious gifts
And now she is angry

Wild storms sweep over lands
That were once calm

Birds, beasts and fish
Her children – are dying

For we have betrayed her
And her beautiful legacy

The goddess guides us
Revealing the miracle of this world

We ask forgiveness
And she will grant it
In her own mysterious way
With beauty and love

NATURE AND HER
OFFSPRING

30: MAY THIS MORNING

May this morning
Bring you light

May this day
Unfold like a flower

When you step into the air
Let the breeze stroke your cheek
The same messenger
That rides on the roar of the sea
And rages through gentle leaves
In great trees

Over your head
The feathery clouds
In the blue sky
Are wild chariots
Stormy tides
Carrying birds on the wing
Angels and distant dreams

With all this
You are blessed
Before you open the door
Before you leave your bed
And long before you awaken

31: TREE PRAYER

It was a moment of connection
A secret heart pumped
Divine waters
From the deep

I stroked your warmth
My smooth weak hand
Touched brown gnarled skin

I listened for your voice
And heard
The sinuous swirl of the sea
Caught in a glorious green crown
That celebrated the heavens
As you danced on the wind

I heard your silent voice
And was amazed
It spoke without fear
No dread of the axe or the saw
No fright of fire
Or the foolish child
No fear

You died
We took your life
We stole your bones
But you were not afraid

You whispered words of love
Love for the creatures that scuttled at your feet
Love for the birds that sat on your branches
Love for those that rested in your shade
Love for the wind
Love for the rain

Your power overwhelmed me
Your grace was divinity
Your song was the voice of a mother
Sweetly crooning to her child

32: THERE WAS A TREE

There was a tree
That stood tall and proud in the rain forest
Home to a thousand families and more
Monkeys had lived in it for generations
They laughed and played on its kindly boughs
Humming birds nested in its branches
And ants, colourful beetles and exquisite
butterflies
Dwelt there too

At the top of the tree the sun shone
Dancing on glittering leaves
And birds sang at dawn
Heralding the start of a God given day
Far below, it was shady
Little mammals scuttled to shelter
Safe in gnarled roots

There was a tree
And a thousand, thousand others
They were home to a myriad families
That laughed and chattered
and played on great branches

for ten thousand years or more
But they have long departed

The music of nature has gone
There is silence
For mile, upon mile, upon mile
A giant savannah
Bears witness to the mind of man

The spirits of the trees are no more
The songs of the glittering birds have gone
The laughter of the monkeys is a memory
And the cowboy drives lumbering livestock
Across a lonely plain
Livestock that lives to die
Die and be consumed
Reconstituted flesh
Served in white pulp
Packed to feed bellies
In a cement filled world

When we are blind to the beauty
When we deaf to the trees
When we do not feel the joy
of the chattering monkey or the birdsong
We lose ourselves

So let us pray for the trees
And for ourselves
For we are as one

33: WINTER

The brooding sun is low and likes to hide
The waxing moon gleams bright on chilly frost
We see your wisdom and your work
We voyage intrepidly beyond the darkening days

Some birds have flown to far-off sunny lands
Some beasts sleep deep beneath your icy spell
We touch the cold and gaze at twinkling stars
Marvelling at winter's shining dance of light

The birds at home sing bravely, in the
morning murk
Their voices trill, and resonate, like bells
We hear your music ringing through the hall
Chanting in celebration – breathing breathy mists

Warm embers in the grate bear memories of
summer's heat
Beyond the door, there's cold and dark
and gloom
We thank you for the wind and rain and snow
The winter solstice, Northern star, the moon

We reach out for your blessing
East and West
And turn in homage
North and South

Now let us pray, and celebrate this time and place
Light the candle, bring radiance to heart and home
Adorn green leaves and berries red as rust
And laugh and love this season, dark and dusk

We are your servants
We give our hearts to those we love and know
And give our thoughts and minds and more
To souls, and beasts and spirits, far beyond the door
We willingly give
As you give to us
We lovingly serve
As you love us

We love, as you love us
And thank you
For the blessing of winter

34: BLESS THIS GREY DAY

Bless this grey day
The sky is covered
But behind the cloud
Is sun and blue sky

Bless the gloom and dreariness
That I see and feel
In this most physical of worlds

I feel the darkness
On one side
The wall of cloud
The physical world
Dull, hidden, shadowy
On the other side
Unseen but accepted
The radiance of spirit
Like the hidden blue

Then, when least expected
The sun breaks through
And shines on us all
Bringing untold joy -
Light, love and laughter

Bless the gloom
For the sun that follows

35: TO THE AIR

Spirits of the air
Riders of the wind
I hear you
And marvel
Your invisible powers
Are for all to see

Your song is beautiful and terrible
As you rage across the white wastes
Of this, our beautiful planet
Your siren music shrieks
Across the Tundra

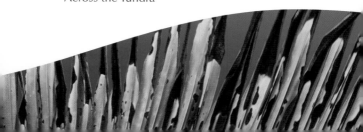

Howls across the manicured
Lawns and condos of Florida
Whipping the leaves of palm trees
Whisking froth on giant seas
Screaming and diving
North, South, East and West
A reminder of our weakness

But on sunny days
In gentle meadows
Resting on a hot beach
We welcome your touch
Your perfect breeze
Cool, loving and gentle
And we thank you

36: EARTH PRAYER

Our mother
Who lies in the soil
Hallowed be thy name
Blacker than night
We rest in your embrace

Here, everywhere and nowhere
Your wisdom is indefinable
Below ground and on high
You reign supreme
Your mysteries unseen

Out of the mud springs the radiant flower
The bright green shoot.
From the filth of grimy grit
Emerges perfection
The five fold star
The petal of fragility
Fine as the wing of a butterfly
Exquisite as a rainbow

We, like you are the stuff of stars
And we like you
Shall turn, and turn
And turn again
Returning as spirits
As stars – as light
As life – as harmony
Pure, innocent
Happy and open
Ready to learn once more

37: THE EARTH IS YOURS AND MINE

The earth is yours and mine
And the glorious sky
As you made me
So you made the starling
And the owl
The glorious oak and elm

In weaving your wisdom
You formed the sea
And her melodious song
Harmonising with the whale and the bird

You are in me
And above me
You are below me
And beside me

You created worlds within worlds
Gifts beyond understanding
Beauty beyond measure
Captured in a sphere of perfect blue

And so we bow to you
Call upon angels and spirits
In the leaves and borne on the air
Implore you
With power
And glory
To give us strength
That we may share
In worship and wisdom this day
Let's join in mind, and spirit
In prayer and love to bring healing
To this most beautiful of worlds
For when this world suffers, we suffer
For we are all as one

ACKNOWLEDGEMENTS

Special thanks to Sue Smallwood, for her wonderful design. Also thanks to Claire Shelton-Jones for introducing me to a different way of writing.

I must also say thanks to Annelise Kean for her interest and passion and the Rev Mary Gavin for her incisive observation, comment and wit.

Thanks also to Marilyn Deegan, for her ideas about punctuation.

Photographs: A selection of the author's own, and others ©1997 PhotoDisc Inc